Gardening
WHICH?

GROWING
BETTER
PLANTS

**The *Gardening. Which?* guide to
choosing composts and feeds to get
the most from container plants**

D1513406

CONTENTS

INTRODUCTION

Whether you are an experienced gardener raising plants from seeds and cuttings or a beginner creating your first hanging basket, your plants will grow faster and flower longer if they are growing in the right compost.

The advice in this booklet is based on the results of scientific tests and trials carried out by *Gardening Which?* over the last ten years. These tests have proved, time and again, that choosing the right compost is critical if you want to grow healthy plants.

A visit to any garden centre or DIY superstore will tell you that there is a vast range of composts for sale. Many are described as 'multipurpose' or 'all-purpose' composts, while others are sold for more specific tasks such as raising seeds and cuttings or for use in hanging baskets and containers. Will a task-specific compost give you better results than a multipurpose one? **This booklet has the answer**.

You will also find 'green' composts on sale. These products contain no peat and are based on recycled materials such as composted bark and timber waste. How does their performance compare with traditional composts? **This booklet has the answer**.

Before peat-based composts became popular, most gardeners used the soil-based John Innes range. Many gardeners still swear by these composts, but how do they compare with the modern peat-based ones? **This booklet has the answer**.

SUCCESS WITH SEEDS

Raising plants from seed is great fun. It's also the cheapest way to fill your garden with flowers and vegetables. Successfully raising plants this way has nothing to do with being 'green fingered'. It's simply a matter of using the right materials and following a few rules.

Which compost?

Choosing the right compost to sow your seeds in is a critical factor in their success or failure. Your options are:

- a peat-based multipurpose compost
- a peat-free multipurpose compost
- a soil-based John Innes seed compost
- a peat-based seed and cutting compost

Tests carried out for *Gardening Which?* over the last ten years have shown that a good-quality, peat-based multipurpose compost is likely to give you the best results. As well as producing the best plants, good multipurpose composts are inexpensive, light and easy to handle.

Some gardeners have reservations about using composts that contain peat for environmental reasons, but tests have shown that the quality of peat-free ones is extremely variable. Recent tests have suggested that peat-free composts are a safer choice now than previously, with some being almost as good as the best peat-based ones. (See page 34 for information on peat-free composts.)

Steps to sowing success

● Fill the seed tray with compost, removing any fibrous lumps, then gently firm it down.

● Stand the seed tray in about 1cm (½in) of water until the surface becomes moist (darkens), then allow to drain.

● Sow the seeds as evenly as possible on the surface of the compost and cover them with sieved compost (check the seed packet for sowing depth). Some seeds need light to germinate so cover these with vermiculite.

● Place in a well-lit spot out of direct sunlight (check seed packet for recommended germination temperature).

Spread the compost out in the seed tray and firm gently

Scatter the seed evenly over the surface of the compost

Very fine seed

For an even spread of very fine seed, such as begonias and lobelias, mix the seed with a small amount of silver sand or vermiculite (see page 46) before sowing. Cover the tray after sowing with clinging film to stop the surface drying out.

Carefully cover the seed with sieved compost

Pricking out

As soon as seedlings have developed leaves and are large enough to handle, they should be transplanted. Don't hold them by their stems as this can have fatal consequences. Instead, lift each seedling carefully by a leaf, while supporting the roots with a pencil or dibber.

Potting on

As seedlings grow, they need to be potted on into larger containers to give their roots room to develop and to give the growing plants access to fresh supplies of nutrients. Pot seedlings on into individual containers of multipurpose compost measuring 7.5-10cm (3-4in) in diameter. Move young plants to their final position (if they are to be planted outdoors) as soon as the risk of frost has passed.

When pricking out, hold each seedling by a leaf and support the delicate root system. Never hold a seedling by the stem

PROBLEM SOLVERS

Growing plants from seed can be hugely satisfying when it works – and extremely frustrating when it doesn't. Below you'll find solutions to some common problems.

What temperature should I sow at?
There is a common misconception that the higher the temperature, the quicker seeds will germinate and the faster the young plant will grow.

In fact, for most seeds a germination temperature of around 15°C (60°F) is best. Any cooler and germination can become slow and erratic – any higher and seedlings can develop too quickly and become weak and leggy. Some plants, such as celery, cyclamen, freesia and lettuce won't even germinate at temperatures above 18°C (65°F).

It will only be beneficial to turn up the heat for seeds from tropical and sub-tropical plants. Cacti, impatiens, cucumber and foliage houseplants all germinate better at around 21°C (70°F). In general, a sunny window-sill in a heated room is a better bet than an airing cupboard. Always follow the instructions on the back of the seed packet carefully to ensure the best results.

How much light is necessary?
Most seeds will germinate equally well in light or dark, but there are a number of important exceptions.

Seeds that are best germinated in light are generally the very fine ones, including African violets, ageratum, antirrhinum, begonia, *Bellis perennis*, celery, *Senecio cineraria*, gloxinia, impatiens, kalanchoë, lobelia, mimulus, nicotiana, petunia, primula and salvia.

Seeds best germinated in the dark include cyclamen, *Eccremocarpus scaber*, nigella, mesembryanthemum, nemesia, *Phlox drummondii* and verbena.

Why do seeds germinate unevenly?

It's frustrating to find seedlings emerging in patches rather than evenly over the whole seed tray. This tends to happen because the seeds have been sown at slightly different depths. When sowing in pots or trays, use a block of wood or the base of a clean flower pot to create a level surface for sowing. To cover the seed to an even depth, sieve compost over the surface and gently firm it down.

When sowing outdoors, create a uniform surface on which to sow by covering the soil with a thin layer of sieved soil mixed with multipurpose compost and firm this down lightly with a block of wood.

How far apart should seeds be sown?

If you're sowing in pots or trays to prick out later, the objective is to produce strong seedlings that are easy to separate. Most seedlings should be spaced about 1cm (½in) apart, but large seeds need to be 2.5cm (1in) apart.

With outdoor sowings in a seed bed for later transplanting, sow all seeds about 3cm (1½in) apart. If they aren't going to be transplanted, aim for about half the final spacing to allow for failures.

With seeds that are known to be erratic in their germination (eg parsnips) or seeds which are sown at a wide spacing (eg beans), it's best to sow three or four seeds together and then thin out the seedlings as they develop into plants.

Why do some seedlings flop?

Seedlings that flop usually do so as a result of a 'damping off' disease. This is a fungal infection which results in the stems becoming thin at soil level so that the seedlings topple over and die – often in circular patches. You may also see a white mould on the compost surface.

To prevent damping off, always wash your pots or seed trays before use and always use fresh compost. Sow as thinly as possible. Use tap water rather than water from a butt. Water from below to avoid wetting seedlings.

Why do some seedlings shrivel?

Lack of water is the main reason why seedlings shrivel up. Keeping the compost evenly moist is the solution. Stand pots and trays in shallow water until the compost surface appears wet then allow them to drain before sowing the seed. With most seeds, you should not need to water again until they germinate. After germination, place trays and pots on damp capillary matting to keep the compost moist.

How much sun should seedlings be given?

Seedlings can be given full sun until mid-March in the South and mid-April in the North. After this, shade them from strong sun which can scorch them. The main problem with window-ledges is that the seedlings tend to lean towards the sun. Turn them every day.

SUCCESS WITH CUTTINGS

If you see a plant in a friend's garden that you'd love in your own, or have a plant in your garden that's seen better days, why not take a cutting during the summer months and grow a new plant?

Which compost?
Most plants are fairly easy to root from cuttings, but the type of compost you grow them in will have a significant impact on how well and how quickly they root.
There are three main choices:
● a multipurpose compost
● a seed and cutting compost
● a DIY mixture of ingredients.

Tests carried out for *Gardening Which?* have shown that multipurpose composts tend to give better results than many seed and cutting composts, but the best results are usually achieved by growing your cuttings in rockwool or a DIY compost mixture. Three DIY mixes that have given good results are:
● a 50:50 mix of multipurpose compost and coarse grit
● a 50:50 mix of multipurpose compost and perlite
● a 50:50 mix of multipurpose compost and sharp sand.

What all three additives have in common is that they improve drainage, so there is less chance of the compost getting saturated and the cuttings rotting. (See page 46 for information on these and other compost additives available from garden centres.)

Should I use rooting hormone?

Plants manufacture their own hormone to promote rooting, so is it really worth dipping cuttings in a man-made version too? Our tests suggest that the answer is 'yes'. While it is true to say that cuttings from some plants will root just as well without, cuttings from many plants seem to root more quickly if they are dipped in a man-made hormone rooting powder.

Some gardeners believe that splitting the base of a cutting before potting it up helps rooting. This is worth trying, but is not essential in our experience.

Tip a little hormone rooting powder into a saucer before dipping in cuttings to prevent contamination. Make sure all the cut surface is covered and shake off excess

HOW TO TAKE CUTTINGS

You can take cuttings from a wide range of plants, including shrubs. The techniques involved are straightforward and no specialist equipment is needed.

Shrub cuttings

Cuttings of different shrubs can be taken throughout the year. Softwood cuttings are those taken in May and June from young shoots before they start to become woody. Semi-ripe cuttings are those taken in mid to late summer just as the current season's shoots start to harden at the base. Hardwood cuttings are those taken in autumn and winter from the past season's growth.

Gardening Which? trials have shown that many rose varieties can be raised successfully from cuttings

Taking softwood cuttings

● Select healthy, non-flowering shoots and remove them with a sharp knife. Put the cuttings in a plastic bag and keep them out of the sun to prevent wilting.

● Trim the cuttings to size and remove the lower leaves.

● Dip the cutting in rooting hormone, shaking off any excess.

Use a clean, sharp blade when taking cuttings

● Push up to six cuttings around the edge of a 10cm (4in) pot. Many cuttings taken in spring and summer can be rooted under a plastic bag. Use sticks or hoops of wire to support the bag, and seal it below the rim of the pot with an elastic band.

● Place pots somewhere warm and out of direct sunlight. Check cuttings from time to time to make sure the compost has not dried out – stand the pot in water for a short while if this happens.

Remove lower leaves before inserting around edge of a pot

● Once you see signs of new root growth, ventilate the cuttings by puncturing the bag to let in more air. When the young plants have hardened off, pot them up individually.

Cover pot with a polythene bag. Secure with rubber band

13

Carefully tear each cutting with a 'heel' at the base

Shake off excess rooting powder before inserting

Taking semi-ripe cuttings

● Select healthy shoots that have started to go woody at the base (turning brown).

● Tear each cutting from the parent plant so that it produces a short 'heel' at the base of the cutting. Put cuttings in a polythene bag.

● Trim the 'heel' with a sharp knife so that there are no rough snags. Dip the base of each cutting in hormone rooting powder and shake off excess.

● Push up to six cuttings around the edge of a 10cm (4in) pot. Cover with a polythene bag and seal it below the rim of the pot with an elastic band.

● Place pots somewhere warm.

Root softwood cuttings in water
Push the cuttings through holes in a polystyrene tile and float this in the surface of an old ice cream tub filled with water. Change the water regularly. The cuttings will be ready for potting on when well-rooted.

Taking hardwood cuttings

● Select stems that are about pencil-thickness and trim them to around 20-30cm (10-12in) in length. With deciduous shrubs, wait until the leaves fall.

● Remove any soft growth at the top of the stem and trim the top at a slight angle so that it sheds the rain. With evergreens and semi-evergreens leave the top three or four leaves.

Trim pencil-thick cuttings to length with secateurs

● Select a reasonably sunny site with well-drained soil. Then, using a spade, make a V-shaped furrow to the depth of the cuttings so that one side is vertical. Line the bottom of the furrow with sharp sand. Then space the cuttings 7.5-15cm (3-6in) apart depending on vigour.

Insert cuttings two-thirds of their length into the furrow

● Insert the cuttings to two-thirds of their length so that they sit on the sand against the vertical side of the furrow. Replace the excavated soil and firm well.

● Keep the area around cuttings well weeded and water them in dry weather. They should be ready for transplanting by the following autumn.

Firm down excavated soil around cuttings

15

Alternative techniques

There are a number of other methods that can be used to root hardwood cuttings if you don't have room for the traditional methods or live in a cold part of the country.

● Bundles of hardwood cuttings can be rooted in a greenhouse or garage by standing them vertically in a bucket of sand. Half fill the bucket with coarse sand, and insert a bundle of cuttings. Overwinter the cuttings indoors but move them outside once the frost becomes less severe.

● Bundles of short cuttings can also be rooted in old growing bags that you have been using during the summer to grow tomatoes in. Flood the compost first with water and let it drain. Wrap the growing bag in a black plastic bin bag and then make some drainage holes in the bottom to stop the cuttings getting waterlogged. Insert the cuttings

In Gardening Which?
trials, bundles of
hardwood cuttings
rooted well in a bucket
of water

16

through the black plastic into pre-cut holes in the growing bag. Rooting should take around three months.

● Water is also a good growing medium for rooting hardwood cuttings. Simply tape a bundle together and stand them upright in a bucket of water. The water should come half way up each cutting, with any leaves held well clear of the water. Change the water every few days, especially as daylength increases in spring.

Store the bucket under a bench in a greenhouse or garage over winter. Once the cuttings have rooted, pot them up in compost.

Tips for success with cuttings

● Take cuttings from well-watered, vigorously growing plants, avoiding flowering shoots.

● Make cuts with a sharp blade – do not use secateurs as these tend to crush the cutting stem.

● Never allow cuttings to wilt or dry out. Spray them with water as soon as you've taken them and keep them out of direct sun and strong light. Most cuttings root better in a humid environment (eg, under a clear polythene bag).

● Cut off any of the cutting's leaves or thorns that will be buried by the compost or touch its surface – otherwise they will rot .

● Keep the compost moist but not sodden.

● Pot cuttings on as soon as they have rooted to encourage rapid growth.

SUCCESS WITH HANGING BASKETS

Hanging baskets can brighten up walls and fences all through the year. But with a lot of plants crammed into a small container and all of them relying on you to keep them fed and watered, your choice of compost is critical.

Which compost?
You have the choice of buying a multipurpose compost or one formulated specifically for hanging baskets.

Get the combination of compost, plants and care right, and you can achieve eye-catching colourful displays that will last all summer

Tests have shown that you are likely to get equally good results from both if you choose the right brand, but multi-purpose ones are usually cheaper.

Which basket and bracket?

Since the basket and bracket are the only parts that can be reused from year to year, it is worth choosing carefully. The bigger the basket you use, the better the displays you will achieve and the easier they will be to look after. A 35cm (14in) or 40cm (16in) diameter one would be ideal, giving masses of colour and only needing watering once a day at most in dry weather.

Smaller baskets (25-30cm/10-12in) tend to dry out very quickly because they contain only a small amount of compost (3-5 litres), and will need watering twice a day in dry weather. The size of bracket you choose will be determined by the size of your basket – heavy-duty metal ones are needed to support the weight of larger baskets.

Which liner?

Hanging baskets have traditionally been lined with sphagnum moss, but in recent years conservation organisations have expressed concerns about a natural resource being used in this way.

If you want to use a man-made product instead, there

are a variety of liners available to hold the compost and plants in position in the basket. A wool felt liner is a good option – these are pre-cut so are easy to plant up and won't look too obtrusive when the basket is first hung.

Which feed?
Hanging baskets need regular feeding. The convenient way to do this is to add a slow-release fertiliser to the compost when you plant the basket up. The other option is to apply a liquid feed at regular intervals.

Both options should give good results, so choose the one that best suits the way you garden. Slow-release fertilisers are more convenient to use if you tend to forget to feed your baskets, but liquid ones are a lot cheaper. Liquid feed any display that is starting to flag.

The most convenient way to feed a hanging basket is to add a slow-release fertiliser to the compost when planting. Liquid feed towards the end of the season if the display starts to flag

How to cut down on watering

Keeping a hanging basket watered in summer can be a time-consuming business. Smaller baskets need most frequent attention, and can need watering as much as twice a day in very hot weather. You can reduce your basket's thirst by doing the following:

● Choose a large basket and drought-tolerant plants.
● Line porous-sided baskets with polythene before planting up.
● Mix some water-retaining gel into the compost unless it contains some already.
● Make watering easier by using a hose lance or water individual baskets with an old drinks bottle.
● Move plants to a shady position during weekdays.

Use a hose lance to make watering hanging baskets easier

SUCCESS WITH SUMMER CONTAINERS

Pots full of brightly-coloured bedding plants bring patios to life during the summer months. To get the best displays, it is important to choose the right compost and allow time for watering and feeding.

Which compost?
You have three basic choices here – multipurpose compost, John Innes compost or tub/hanging basket compost. But there are a number of other factors to consider – cost in particular.

Fuchsia, lobelia and helichrysum 'Limelight' combine in this colourful display

You can get equally good results from all three if you choose the right brand but multipurpose ones are usually cheaper.

Also consider buying growing bags and use the compost from these. Growing bags are generally around half the price of multipurpose compost but will produce quite acceptable displays over one season. You could also consider using your garden soil, as long as it is not sticky clay or very chalky.

Which feed?

Summer containers filled with bedding plants and other tender specimens need regular feeding to produce good, long-lasting displays. The most convenient way to do this

Tender perennials zantedeschia (right) and solenopsis

is to add a slow-release fertiliser to the compost when you plant the containers up. The other option is to apply a liquid feed regularly (check the manufacturer's instructions for frequency).

Liquid feeds are the cheaper option and our tests have shown that they are likely to give the best results, but they don't suit everybody. If you tend to forget to feed your baskets or are away from home a lot in summer, a slow-release fertiliser is best for you.

Which container?

Clay and terracotta pots are an attractive choice for summer patio displays. Bear in mind, though, that they are more expensive than plastic ones and heavier to move. They also allow water to evaporate through their sides, so need more frequent watering in hot weather. You can

Prevent water evaporating from terracotta pots by lining them with polythene

reduce the evaporation rate by lining the insides of terracotta pots with polythene before planting.

Plastic pots are cheaper, lighter to carry around and need less watering – but don't look so attractive. If you like the terracotta look, but want the convenience of plastic, either buy terracotta look-alikes made from plastic or buy one or two terracotta pots for prominent spots and plastic ones elsewhere.

Attractive terracotta pot overflowing with petunias and lobelias

---

Tips for success

● Putting crocks in the bottom of containers to improve drainage is not essential if you use good quality compost, though they do add stability.

● Cover large drainage holes to prevent the compost being washed out as you water.

● Use an old compost bag or black polythene bin liner to help retain moisture in terracotta pots during the summer months.

● Positioning containers in partial shade will reduce the need for frequent watering.

● Plant up one or two spare pots to allow for failures.

WATERING MADE EASY

Keeping containers and hanging baskets watered in summer can quickly become hard work. Instead of being able to sit back and enjoy the fruits of your labours, you can find yourself spending as much as an hour a day with a watering can in your hand.

In the past, many gardeners have used devices such as sprinklers to water their gardens for them, but these are now seen as water-wasters. The modern alternative is a system of interconnecting hoses controlled by a simple water 'computer'. Such a system is capable of watering borders and vegetable plots as well as containers and hanging baskets and can be programmed to carry on watering at set times of the day or night even when you are away on holiday.

The main components of any domestic automatic watering system are:

● seephoses
● drip systems
● water computers.

Seephoses
Seephoses are the most efficient way to water large areas of the garden such as

Use a drip system to water individual pots and hanging baskets

herbaceous borders and vegetable or fruit plots. They lie on the surface of the soil or can be buried just below the surface, with water seeping out of tiny holes all along their length for a fixed amount of time.

Drip systems
These are best suited to individual plants in containers or greenhouses. Fine tubes branch off a main hosepipe, each ending in a nozzle which drips water into a single pot or hanging basket. Drip systems and seephoses can be linked together and controlled by a single water computer.

Water computers
These are attached to an outside tap. They run on batteries rather than mains electricity, so you don't need to worry about safety or get involved in any complex wiring jobs. Some are fairly basic and can only turn themselves on and off once a day. Others are more sophisticated and can operate up to six on/off cycles in a 24-hour period. None is hard to programme – if you can cope with a central heating timer, you can handle a water computer.

At the end of the summer, all pipes should be drained off to avoid any problems with frost, and the ends should be plugged so that dirt cannot get in. At the start of the next season, simply flush the system through.

If you live in a hard water area, you may find that after a while drip systems start to become blocked up with limescale. This can be cleared out with a limescale remover (available from supermarkets), just as you would a shower head in the bathroom.

SUCCESS WITH YEAR-ROUND CONTAINERS

Containers planted with colourful shrubs and small trees make superb focal points in the garden. They can be particularly useful in autumn, winter and spring when the rest of the garden is bare.

Which compost?
For best results it is essential to choose a good-quality compost that will perform well over several years, not just a few months. Year-round containers are exposed to drought, frost and excessive wet. The compost you choose

Permanent planting of spotted laurel and trailing variegated ivy is supplemented in summer with a bright splash of pink pelargoniums

must be able to cope with all of these, without losing its structure, and continue to supply a balanced mixture of nutrients to the plants growing in them.

You have four choices:
- a multipurpose peat-based compost
- a multipurpose peat-free compost
- a peat-based container compost
- a soil-based John Innes compost.

Tests have shown that the best results are usually achieved with a good-quality peat-based multipurpose or container compost. Multipurpose composts are usually cheaper. John Innes composts are only worth considering if you want to make the pot heavier and less likely to blow over.

Which container?

If you are going to use clay or terracotta pots, line them with polythene to reduce moisture loss. If you live in an exposed spot that's prone to hard frosts, line the pot with insulating bubble polythene to reduce the risk of the pot cracking over winter. Mock-terracotta pots made of plastic are a lot cheaper and lighter and won't crack in frost. Many

Elegant clipped box with a spring display of pansies and dwarf narcissi

look almost as good as the real thing, especially once they have been planted up. Wooden half-barrels are also worth considering. Look for solidly constructed ones, held together by sturdy metal bands. If you choose one that doesn't have a drainage hole in the bottom, drill one.

Which feed?

Feeding permanent containers is essential as the compost in which the plants are growing will quickly run out of nutrients. Check the compost packaging for the manufacturer's recommendation as to when to start feeding.

You can feed plants using either a liquid fertiliser or a slow-release one. Liquid fertilisers are cheaper, but slow-release ones are more convenient to use.

If you opt for a liquid feed, apply it throughout the summer months. Gradually reduce feeding during August and stop by the end of the month. This will prevent the

Simple and attractive: a single specimen of the dwarf pine Pinus 'Mugo'

plants producing a lot of soft gworth during the autumn which will then be vulnerable to frost damage.

Slow-release fertiliser granules are sold in a range of formulations - some last up to a year. They produce reasonable results with most plants, but fast-growing specimens will give better displays if you treat them to a supplementary liquid feed.

Winter interest with dwarf narcissi, vinca, skimmia, lavender and hebe

---

Tips for success

● Grow plants in the largest container you can.

● Group containers together so the plants create a moist microclimate around their leaves and shade the compost from sun in summer.

● If you are planting a large specimen, position it in its original pot inside the new container on a layer of compost. Then fill the new container with compost while the original pot is still in place. Firm the compost round the edges and then remove the original pot. Plant the specimen in the hole left behind.

● Water containers in early morning or evening in summer rather than in the heat of the day to reduce the rate of evaporation.

SUCCESS WITH ERICACEOUS PLANTS

Rhododendrons and azaleas produce spectacular flowers in spring and early summer, but the soil in many gardens is not acidic enough for them. Heavy clay soils, and light sandy ones are not to their liking either.

The best way to grow these, and other ericaceous plants such as camellias, is in containers, which you can fill with a compost more to their liking. Growing shrubs such as rhododendrons in pots also helps contain their growth – particularly important in smaller gardens – and means you can move them to prominent positions in the garden when they are looking their best.

Which compost?

You will find specialist ericaceous composts on sale in garden centres, but our tests have shown that these are not necessarily the best buy for ericaceous plants.

Some good-quality multipurpose composts have given us just as good a result – and can be considerably cheaper to buy.

Acid-loving dwarf rhododendrons grow well in a pot

Which feed?

Ericaceous plants in containers need regular feeding during the summer months when they are actively growing. Use a balanced liquid feed or a slow-release fertiliser.

Watering

Rainwater from a water butt is ideal for acid-loving plants in containers. Tap water is also suitable if you live in a soft water area. If you live in a hard water area, using tap water will gradually make the compost more alkaline and the plants will start to look sickly.

If you live in a hard water area and don't have a water butt, water your plants with a weak solution of ammonium sulphate dissolved in tap water (about a level teaspoon per 4.5litres/one gallon of water).

If after one or two growing seasons you find the leaves of your plants starting to turn yellow, increase the amount of ammonium sulphate in the water by a half.

If this doesn't work, either try to find room in your garden for a water butt to collect rainwater or try repotting the plants into an ericaceous compost to see if this does the trick.

Pernettya, lamium, erica, ivy and primula make a colour-themed container

33

PEAT-FREE COMPOSTS

Over the last few years, pressure has been growing on gardeners to help preserve peatland habitats by using alternatives to peat.

Peat bogs are found all over the world, but each forms under different environmental conditions and has its own unique flora and fauna combination. Harvesting the peat on a commercial scale inevitably disrupts the balance of nature and threatens the future of rare plants and wildlife.

According to recent figures, gardeners use about one million tonnes of peat a year. It is used in three ways:

- as a general soil improver
- as a mulch to retain moisture and suppress weeds
- as an ingredient in compost.

Using peat as a soil improver makes no sense – farmyard manure is much cheaper and more effective. The same can be said for using it as a mulch – you'd be better off using grass clippings.

Which leaves composts. In recent years a number of peat-free composts have appeared in garden centres based on materials such as wood waste and coir, a by-product produced from coconuts. *Gardening Which?* has been testing them since 1991 in an attempt to find one that really works. In our early trials many peat-free composts produced very inferior plants to peat-based composts but recent trials have identified some which are almost as good as the best peat-based ones. We are concerned that gardeners who get bad results from peat-free composts now will be reluctant to try them again.

Feeding peat-free composts
Even the best composts contain only enough nutrients to keep plants happy for about six weeks. For bark- and coir-based composts, the figure is sometimes only three to four weeks so check the feeding information on the bag.

There are now liquid fertilisers available which have been formulated for plants growing in peat-free composts. However, our tests suggest that you will get as good — if not better — results using your normal feed.

Watering peat-free composts
Coir-based composts tend to look dried out when they aren't Overwatering can put the health of plants at risk, so it's worth taking extra care when deciding how often to water. If the surface of the compost is looking dry, press your finger a couple of inches below the surface and feel how dry – or wet it is. If the compost at this lower level still feels moist, then don't water the plants. If it feels dry at this level, give them a drink.

Bark-based composts do not have the same watering problems as coir-based ones but can dry out quicker than peat-based ones.

SUCCESS WITH HOUSEPLANTS

Houseplants are often regarded as short-term purchases.
Many people buy them in flower, only to throw them away
again as soon as the blooms fade.

This is a great pity – and a great waste of money. If you
treat them in the right way, some houseplants can flourish
for years on window-sills, in porches – even in bathrooms.

Creating the right environment

The two biggest causes of houseplant death aren't pests or
diseases – they are dry, centrally heated air, and draughts.

With the right treatment, this azalea will flower again year after year

This is because many of the plants we grow indoors in this country originate from humid parts of the world such as southern Africa and South America where the temperature is fairly constant all year round. The key to making them feel at home here is to recreate those conditions by keeping the air around them moist and the temperature even.

The most effective way to keep the air around your houseplants moist is to grow them together in a group in a pebble tray – a shallow container with a layer of pebbles in the base kept damp by regular watering.

The tray should be positioned out of draughts and away from direct heat sources such as open fires and radiators. A temperature of around 15°C (60°F) is ideal for most common houseplants. Spraying the plants with tepid water also helps to prevent them drying out.

A selection of the more common houseplants on sale over the winter months

Repotting houseplants

Most houseplants benefit from being repotted annually into a larger container. Repotting gives the plants access to fresh nutrients in the new compost and gives the roots more room to grow. Exceptions which prefer to be left undisturbed for several years include African violets, aspidistras, parlour palms and yuccas.

Which compost?

You have two basic choices when picking a houseplant compost: a multipurpose compost or a specialist houseplant compost.

Repotting an African violet

Help ease out plants by pushing from below with a pencil

Use the old pot as a mould when filli the new one with compost

Houseplant composts are generally more expensive than multipurpose ones, but most plants will do just as well in a good-quality multipurpose compost.

When to feed?

For best results, start feeding foliage houseplants once a week in spring and continue feeding throughout the summer. Feeding should not be necessary immediately after repotting, but will need to be resumed 4-12 weeks after repotting, depending on the plant and the compost.

Flowering houseplants should be fed once a week while in bud and flower, but feeding should be stopped when flowering finishes (see 'Giving your houseplants a rest', page 41). Watering should also be reduced when flowering has finished.

remove the inner pot and slip the rootball of the plant into the hole

Which feed?

Our tests have shown that houseplants benefit enormously from regular feeding. The question is 'which one to use?' Traditionally, houseplants have been liquid-fed (feeding while you water), and this remains the best way to tailor feeding to the individual plant's needs. However, for forgetful gardeners there is now a range of slow-release fertilisers for houseplants, which are usually sold as granules.

Most liquid houseplant feeds claim to cater for both flowering and foliage houseplants, but you can also get specialist feeds aimed at non-flowering plants and feeds specifically designed to produce outstanding flowers. Foliar sprays are also available. These are very dilute solutions which you apply directly to the plant's leaves rather than the compost.

In addition to the above, tomato fertilisers are often recommended to improve or extend flowering as they contain high levels of potash.

Our tests suggest that you can achieve good results with either a good-quality liquid feed or a slow-release fertiliser. We have also had good results with tomato feeds.

Use a dual-purpose liquid feed to get best results with both flowering and foliage houseplants

Foliar sprays are only really designed for supplementary feeding of quick-growing or sickly plants. They should not be used on hairy-leaved plants, cacti or ferns as they can damage their foliage.

Giving your houseplants a rest

Virtually all houseplants need a rest period when they recharge their batteries. This is usually in winter when there is less daylight.

It is important to reduce watering at this time of year and to stop feeding altogether for several months. Many plants also prefer a lower temperature during their rest period – move them to a cooler part of the house or even outdoors to a frost-free greenhouse if you live in a mild part of the country.

Capillary matting makes watering pot plants easy

SUCCESS WITH BULBS INDOORS

Indoor bulbs such as hyacinths and hippeastrums can provide spectacular displays of colour during the autumn and winter months when eye-catching garden flowers are in short supply.

What to plant when?

With a little planning, it is possible to have bulbs in bloom from November right through to March. Start in early September by planting prepared hyacinths such as 'Rosalie' or 'Pink Pearl'. In early October, plant mixed

Most bulbs should have 5cm (2in) of compost below them and their tips just showing. For exceptions, see 'Tips for success' page 44

Dutch hybrid crocuses, dwarf irises like *Iris histrioides* 'Major' and 'Paper White' narcissi. Later the same month plant non-prepared hyacinths such as 'Carnegie', *Narcissus* 'Soleil d'Or' and double early tulips, like 'Peach Blossom'. Buy and plant 'Oscar' or other red hippeastrums straight after Christmas.

The resulting flowering sequence should be:

● Early November – pure white, scented narcissi.
● Late November – yellow narcissi with red cups.
● Late December – pink hyacinths.
● Early January – blue dwarf iris.
● Late January – blue and white hyacinths.
● Early February – yellow, white and purple crocus.
● Late February – pink and white tulips.
● Early March – deep red hippeastrums.

Plant up hyacinths as early as September for a fragrant and colourful display in early November

Which compost?

Bulbs can be grown in either a multipurpose compost or a
specialist bulb fibre. Since bulbs contain within them all
the nourishment they need to grow and flower, the quality
of the growing medium is far less important than it is
when you are raising cuttings or seeds. Many bulbs can
actually be grown in water alone, so even their need for a

Tips for success

● Only choose varieties recommended for indoor
growing.

● Use a deep enough bowl to have at least 5cm (2in)
of compost below the bulbs and, for most bulbs, to
allow the tips to just show. Exceptions are
hippeastrums, where the top half of the bulbs should
be exposed, and tulips which should be just covered.

● If using undrained bowls, be careful not to
overwater and add charcoal to the compost.

● Once planted, most bulbs need a period in a cold (5-
7°C/45-48°F) dark place. A shed or garage will do.

● When the shoots start to show, wait for the flower
bud to appear through the neck and do not bring the
bulbs indoors until you can feel it.

● The bulbs then need a light but cool position for a
week or two. Bring the bulbs into the warmth when
the flower buds are well clear of the bulb.
Hippeastrums and hyacinths are most tolerant of
warmth; smaller bulbs do best in cool conditions.

good physical structure is far less than with other plants.

Thirty years ago when most composts were soil-based, peat-based bulb fibre was seen as a clean, lightweight and convenient alternative for indoor use.

However, with peat-based composts now dominating the market, bulb fibre has lost much of its appeal.

Hippeastrums and narcissi thrive on a sunny window-sill

Its main selling point these days is that it contains charcoal to absorb any off-smelling gases which can be produced in bowls without drainage, and crushed egg shells to improve drainage and raise pH.

On trial, bulb fibres have given slightly better results than multipurpose composts, though performance does appear to vary depending on what you want to grow. Hyacinths, for example, seem to grow well in either, whereas narcissi have shown a definite preference for good-quality bulb fibre.

Small bags of bulb fibre are relatively expensive to buy, so if you are planning to fill only one or two bowls, a good-quality multipurpose compost is best value for money. However, if you are planning a large display, opt for bulb fibre.

MIXING YOUR OWN COMPOST

As this booklet makes clear, a good-quality multipurpose compost is the best choice for growing most plants, but there are exceptions. Growing on cuttings is the most obvious example. Tests have shown that the best results are achieved by growing cuttings in rockwool or one of three DIY mixtures:

● a 50:50 mix of multipurpose compost and coarse grit
● a 50:50 mix of multipurpose compost and perlite
● a 50:50 mix of multipurpose compost and sharp sand.

There are several other ingredients that can be used to improve the growth of delicate or fussy plants.

Improving drainage
Sand, grit and gravel are the main ingredients that can be added to compost to improve drainage. They are frequently added to pots containing young plants that would otherwise be at risk from waterlogging, and plants from rocky or arid parts of the world which hate to have their roots sitting in water. Different names are used to refer to different particle sizes:

● silver sand – 1mm particles which are often mixed with fine seed to ensure its even distribution when sowing
● sharp sand – 3mm particles suitable for use in cutting composts

● coarse grit – 4mm particles for use with cuttings and plants which need very free-draining soil to thrive eg, alpines and cacti

● gravel – 6mm particles for use as crocks and for top-dressing small pots

● pea gravel – 5-10mm particles for use as crocks and top-dressing for large pots.

If you see these materials referred to as being 'washed' or 'graded', this means they will have had tiny silt particles removed. Avoid soft 'builders' sand' as this may be too limy or salty for your plants' taste.

Perlite is another popular material for improving drainage. It's made from volcanic rock, which is heated to form white, lightweight granules. Some gardeners prefer to use it instead of sand. When crushed, it can also be used as an alternative to silver sand when sowing fine seed.

Improving water retention

A number of ingredients can be added to compost to improve water retention. Moss peat and sedge peat are the two main ones. Others include vermiculite, a mineral heated to produce lightweight flakes. Coarse-grades can also improve air-holding.

Acid or alkaline?

Acidifiers are added to compost mixes for growing lime-hating plants such as rhododendrons and azaleas. Adding lime to a mix has the opposite effect and makes the mix more palatable to plants such as carnations and some alpines.

Published by Which? Ltd
2 Marylebone Road
London NW1 4DF

Third edition 1999

Copyright © 1999 Which? Ltd

ISBN 0 85202 682 X

Cover design by Creation
Communications

No part of this publication may be reproduced or transmitted in any form or by any means, electronically or mechanically, including photocopying, recording or any information storage or retrieval system, without prior permission in writing from the publisher. This publication is not included under licences issued by the Copyright Agency.

Compiled and edited by
Jonathan Edwards, Martyn Hocking,
Kate Hawkins and Hetty Don.

Printed by WPG Ltd
Welshpool 1999, 01938 556601

MGB23